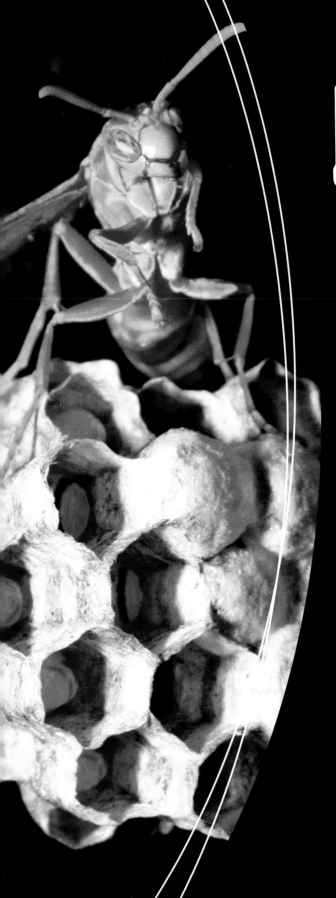

BUGS IN
YOUR HOME

Richard Spilsbury

WAYLAND

First published in 2015 by Wayland
Copyright Wayland 2015

All rights reserved
Dewey number: 578.7'554-dc23
ISBN: 9780750294485
10 9 8 7 6 5 4 3 2 1

Commissioning editor: Victoria Brooker
Project editor: Kelly Davis
Designer: Paul Cherrill for Basement68
Picture research: Richard Spilsbury
   and Alice Harman
Proofreader and indexer: Martyn Oliver

Produced for Wayland by
White-Thomson Publishing Ltd

www.wtpub.co.uk

+44 (0)843 2087 460

Wayland
An imprint of
Hachette Children's Group
Part of Hodder & Stoughton
Carmelite House
50 Victoria Embankment
London EC4Y 0DZ

Picture credits
3 (right), Dreamstime/Sanclemenesdigpro; 6, Science Photo Library/Dr Tony Brain and David Parker; 7 (top), Dreamstime/Dmitry Kalinovsky; 7 (bottom), Shutterstock/Noah Strycker; 8 (top), Dreamstime/Joseph Gough; 8 (bottom), Dreamstime/Inga Nielsen; 9, Science Photo Library/Microfield Scientific Ltd; 10 (left), Dreamstime/Michal Malysa; 10 (right), Dreamstime/Isselee; 11, Science Photo Library/Claude Nuridsany and Marie Perennou; 12, Dreamstime/ Viacheslav Dyachkov; 13, Science Photo Library/David Scharf; 14, Shutterstock/ Birute Vijeikiene; 15, Science Photo Library/Thomas Deerinck, NCMIR; 16, Shutterstock/D. Kucharski and K. Kucharska; 17, Science Photo Library/ Power and Syred; 18, Wikimedia Commons/Gilles San Martin; 19, Science Photo Library/Dr Jeremy Burgess; 20, Dreamstime/Holger Leyrer; 21 (top), Science Photo Library/Power and Syred; 21 (bottom), Alamy/Robert Harding Picture Library Ltd; 22, Dreamstime/Marco Lijo; 23, Science Photo Library/Steve Gschmeissner; 24 (left), Shutterstock/Gucio_55; 24 (right), Jolanta Dabrowska; 25, Science Photo Library/Steve Gschmeissner; 26 (top), Shutterstock/EuToch; 26 (bottom), Shutterstock/Michael Pettigrew; 27 (top), Shutterstock/Robert Adrian Hillman; 27 (bottom), Science Photo Library/Dr Richard Kessel and Dr Gene Shih, Visuals Unlimited; cover, Science Photo Library/Eye of Science.

Printed in China

An Hachette UK company
www.hachette.co.uk
www.hachettechildrens.co.uk

Contents

The scale of things   6

Mouldy old food   8

Nasty housefly habits   10

Creepy cockroaches   12

Spinning spiders   14

Carpet creatures   16

Skin-devouring mites   18

Paper-munching silverfish   20

Nasty wasp nests   22

Wiggly woodworms   24

Termite invaders   26

Glossary   28

Find out more   29

Index   30

The scale of things

At home we are never alone... The places we live in are ideal **habitats** for other living things. But many remain out of sight, or they are so small that we cannot see them without using powerful microscopes to zoom in on them. Then we can see these household horrors up close!

Bacteria are tiny living things that can coat almost every surface in a home. This is the tip of a pin (pink) coated with bacteria (orange).

Invisible world

It's hard to imagine how small some things really are. The smallest objects the human eye can see are about 0.2 mm long. There are 1000 **microns** to a millimetre. A human hair (with a width of about 100 microns) is vast, compared to most things scientists zoom in on!

Sense of scale

A scale tells you how big something is shown, compared to its real size. This is what it means when something is said to be 25 times its actual size. You'll see scales next to many images in this book, to give you a sense of the size of the objects.

These bacteria are
700
TIMES
their actual size

Tools of the trade

Light **microscopes** use **lenses** -- curved pieces of glass -- that bend light rays to magnify an image (make it larger). They bounce light off surfaces to create these images. The most powerful light microscopes can **magnify** things up to about 2000 times. They can even make tiny bacteria visible.

House of horrors?

You'll see some weird and wonderful creatures that share our houses in this book. They might look rather horrific, but don't worry. Some are damaging or even harmful, but most are completely harmless.

A light microscope.

Humans are not the only sort of living thing that is found in our homes...

Scanning electron microscopes (SEMs)

These microscopes use electrons instead of light. (Electrons are tiny parts inside **atoms**.) SEMs bounce electrons off surfaces to create images. Electron microscopes can magnify things by almost a million times!

Mouldy old food

You reach into the bread bin to make a sandwich but - yuck - the loaf is covered with weird fuzzy green spots! What happened?

Mould attack

The bread is covered with **mould**. Mould is not a plant but a **fungus** (like mushrooms or toadstools). It grows by **digesting** plant or animal matter such as leaves, paper, dirt and food. The mould on your bread isn't just on the surface. Its roots are like very thin threads and they spread inside food too. Time to find something else for lunch!

Mould breaks down dead and waste material and recycles it back into the soil.

Mouldy cheese

We usually throw mouldy food away, but some moulds are safe and good to eat. Blue cheeses, such as Gorgonzola and Stilton, have greenish moulds inside. Cheeses like Brie and Camembert have white moulds on the surface.

Stilton gets its tangy taste from the mould it contains.

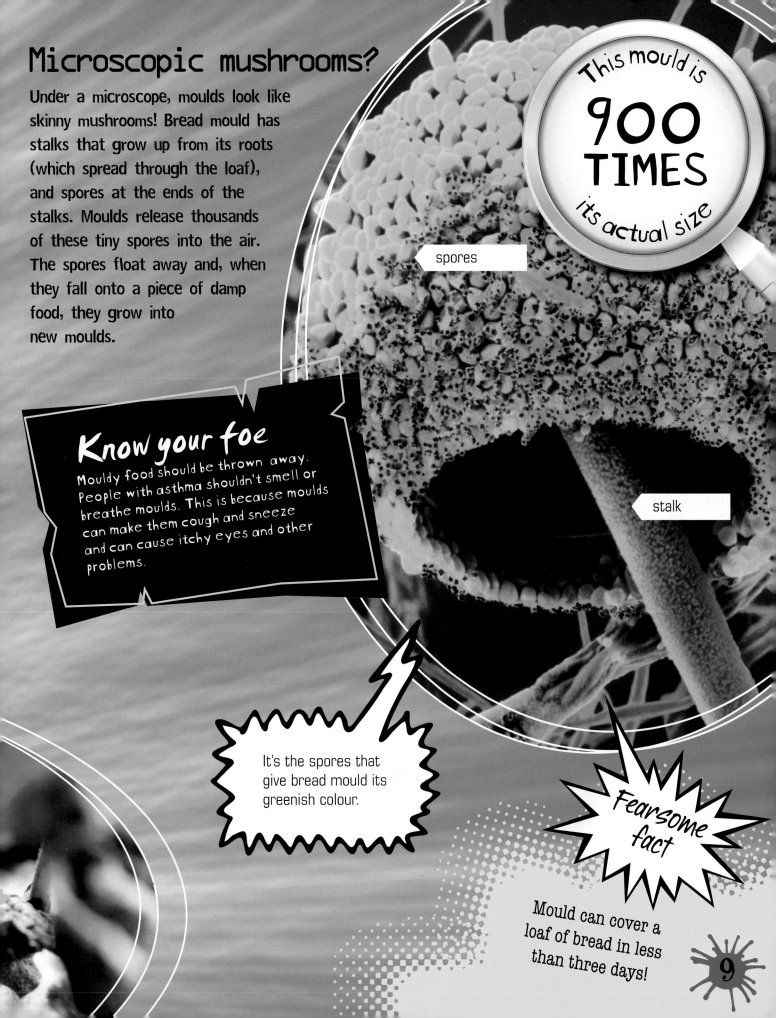

Microscopic mushrooms?

Under a microscope, moulds look like skinny mushrooms! Bread mould has stalks that grow up from its roots (which spread through the loaf), and spores at the ends of the stalks. Moulds release thousands of these tiny spores into the air. The spores float away and, when they fall onto a piece of damp food, they grow into new moulds.

This mould is **900 TIMES** its actual size

spores

stalk

Know your foe

Mouldy food should be thrown away. People with asthma shouldn't smell or breathe moulds. This is because moulds can make them cough and sneeze and can cause itchy eyes and other problems.

It's the spores that give bread mould its greenish colour.

Fearsome fact

Mould can cover a loaf of bread in less than three days!

Nasty housefly habits

Houseflies look pretty harmless, don't they? Maybe so, but if you zoomed in on one it might make your stomach churn!

Dirty habits

Flies aren't fussy eaters. They will dine on dung heaps, rotting food, dead animals — anything that smells good to them. The problem is that, when they land on dirty things, the little hairs all over their body and legs pick up bacteria. Then, when they land on uncovered food, those bacteria rub off onto our dinner! That's not the worst bit. Flies produce faeces (poo) every four or five minutes, usually while they are eating! Fly-swat anyone?

Flies can carry over 100 different kinds of bacteria and other micro-organisms.

Most houseflies live within 3.2 km (2 miles) of where they were born, but will travel up to 32 km (20 miles) to find food!

Bye-bye fly

The easiest way to keep flies out of your home is to keep things clean. Don't leave food lying around, remove rubbish regularly and wipe up messes straight away, especially pet poo!

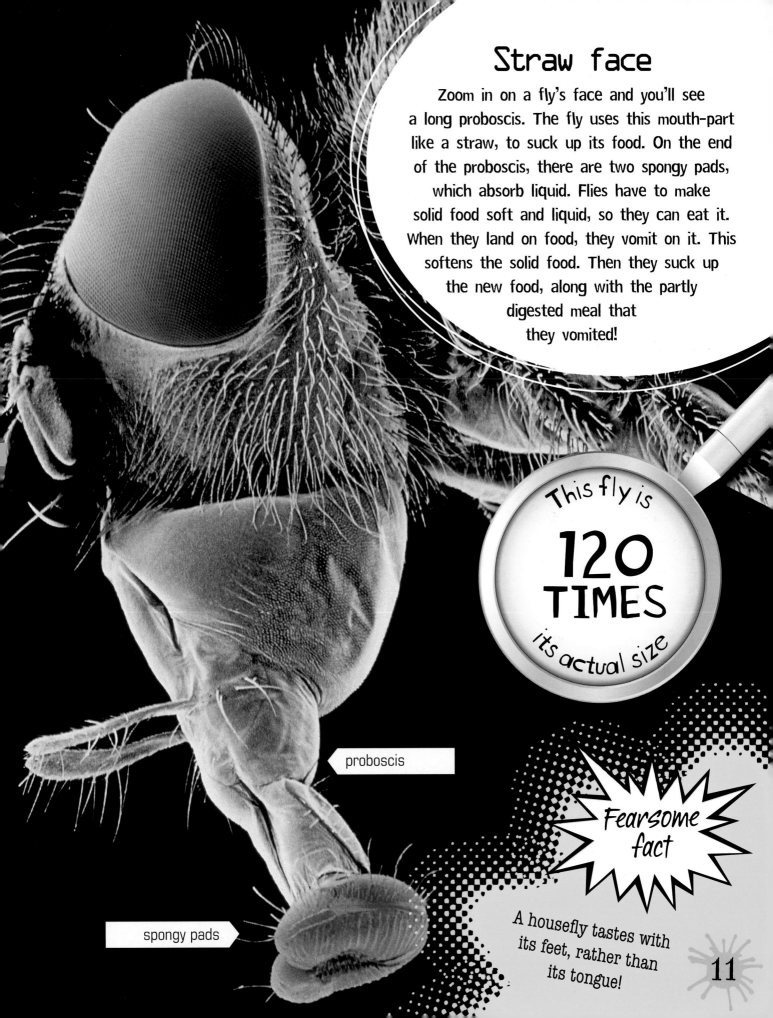

Straw face

Zoom in on a fly's face and you'll see a long proboscis. The fly uses this mouth-part like a straw, to suck up its food. On the end of the proboscis, there are two spongy pads, which absorb liquid. Flies have to make solid food soft and liquid, so they can eat it. When they land on food, they vomit on it. This softens the solid food. Then they suck up the new food, along with the partly digested meal that they vomited!

This fly is

120 TIMES

its actual size

proboscis

spongy pads

Fearsome fact

A housefly tastes with its feet, rather than its tongue!

Creepy cockroaches

If you hear a scuttling sound in the kitchen at night, it may be cockroaches. Shine a torch at these flat, shiny beetles - and they will scuttle away. They don't like light!

Contaminating cockroaches

Cockroaches rest during the day. Their flat bodies allow them to squeeze into the smallest cracks in a kitchen. Then they come out at night to feed. Cockroaches eat almost anything they can find! When they eat our food, they contaminate it with **saliva** (spit) and faeces (poo). Cockroaches can be a pest because they can pass on nasty diseases caused by germs in their faeces.

Perfect pets?

Only about 1 per cent of the 3500 different kinds of cockroach in the world are pests. Some people even keep cockroaches as pets!

Cockroaches usually live near the kitchen so that they can find left-over food to eat.

Know your foe

You don't have to see a cockroach to know they are there. Cockroaches leave a trail of faeces when they move around. The droppings look like tiny coffee granules. The smelly trails guide them to food in the dark.

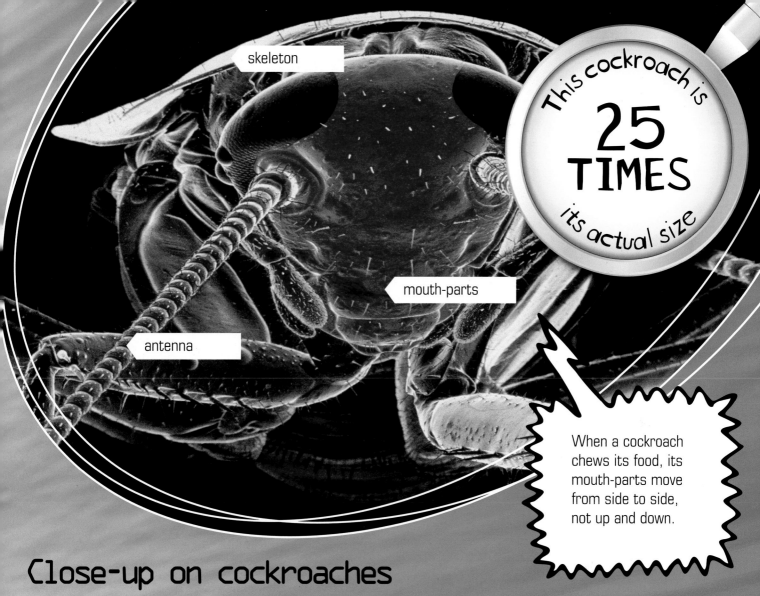

skeleton

antenna

mouth-parts

This cockroach is **25 TIMES** its actual size

When a cockroach chews its food, its mouth-parts move from side to side, not up and down.

Close-up on cockroaches

When you zoom in on a cockroach, you will notice its **antennae**. These give the cockroach its excellent sense of smell. They sweep the air, searching for smells that help them to find food.

The skeleton on the outside of its body protects the cockroach. At the end of each leg it has a double claw and a footpad. These help the cockroach grip surfaces so it can move and climb quickly. It feels things through the hairs on its legs.

Related horrors

The Australian rhinoceros cockroach weighs up to 34 g (1.2 ounces) and is 8 cm (3 inches) long. This big beetle lives more than 10 years. Meanwhile, in Brazil there's a variety of cockroach that is said to eat sleeping people's eyelashes!

Fearsome fact

Cockroaches can live three months without food and even survive explosions!

13

Spinning spiders

Shine a torch in the cellar or garage and you might spot something spinning from the roof. It is a cellar spider, disturbed by the light.

Gangly legs

The cellar spider has very long, skinny, gangly legs. It spins a messy web from silk produced in its cylinder-shaped body. The spider is a **predator** that uses its web to trap **prey**. It dangles upside down, with legs outstretched from its web. It shoots out its front legs to grab animals caught in its web.

Imagine having legs that are five times the length of your body! Cellar spiders are commonly known as daddy-long-legs. (Crane flies are also known by this name.)

> Cellar spiders prefer life out of the spotlight – in the dark, waiting for a meal.

Know your foe

Cellar spiders start spinning from their web when they are disturbed. They actually quiver back and forth on their legs. This means they look blurred to any possible predator, such as a larger spider, which may put off their attacker.

14

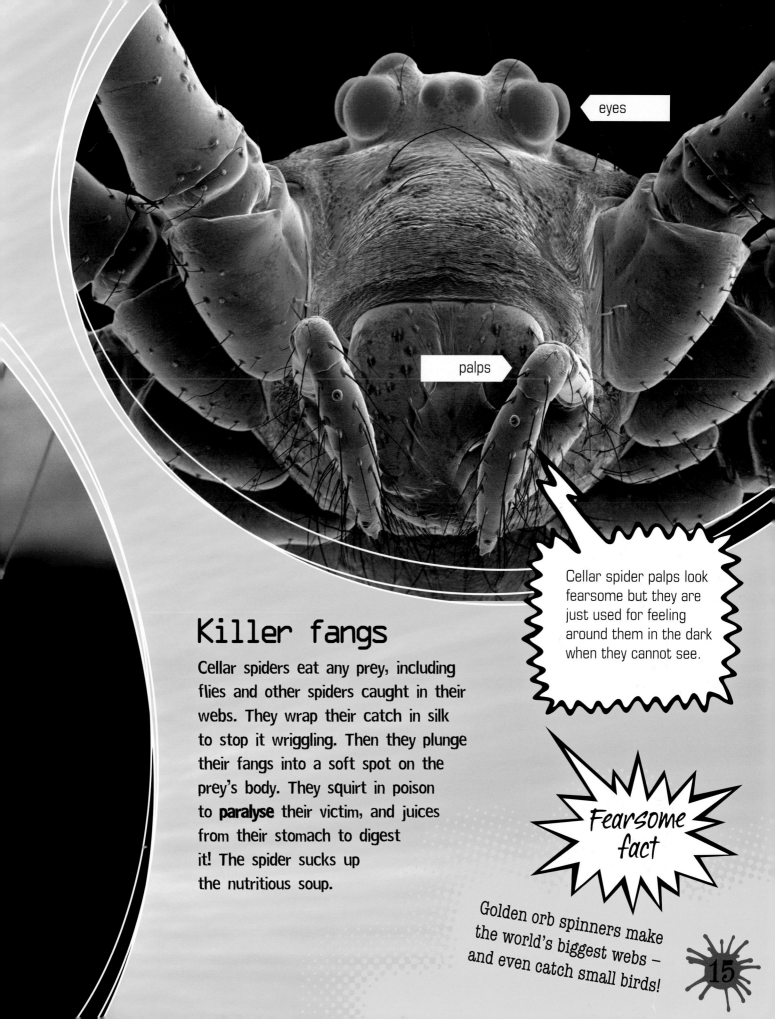

eyes

palps

Killer fangs

Cellar spiders eat any prey, including flies and other spiders caught in their webs. They wrap their catch in silk to stop it wriggling. Then they plunge their fangs into a soft spot on the prey's body. They squirt in poison to **paralyse** their victim, and juices from their stomach to digest it! The spider sucks up the nutritious soup.

Cellar spider palps look fearsome but they are just used for feeling around them in the dark when they cannot see.

Fearsome fact

Golden orb spinners make the world's biggest webs – and even catch small birds!

15

Carpet creatures

Lie down on a carpet and you might imagine that you can hear a faint munching sound. Carpets are a favourite habitat and source of food for carpet beetle **larvae**.

Woolly bears!

Carpet beetles are black, as long as a grain of rice, and harmless. They feed on **nectar** and **pollen** from plants. But their tufty larvae — often called 'woolly bears' — can cause lots of damage. They like nothing better than to feed on **keratin**. This is a natural substance found, for example, in wool, feathers and leather. If left undisturbed, woolly bears can ruin carpets and clothing.

This is a carpet beetle larva, known as a woolly bear.

Know your foe

Carpet beetles often enter houses with the help of birds. When birds make nests in roofs, beetles fly in and lay eggs there. Larvae hatch and feed on feathers, but may also get into the roof and crawl in along water pipes.

Museum beetles

Carpet beetles have small relatives called museum beetles. These cause major damage in museums, for example by eating collections of rare dried butterflies, moths and beetles!

16

These larva hairs are **3000 TIMES** their actual size

Hairy weapons

Some people start scratching or even coughing when their homes have carpet beetles. Zoom in on the tiny hairs on the larva's back and you can see why. The hairs are shaped like spears that can stick into human skin and they may cause rashes and other allergic reactions.

Trapped by smell

Pest controllers set traps containing **pheromone** chemicals that smell of male carpet beetles. Females attracted into the trap to mate with males are killed by **pesticides** there. Without females, there are no eggs and no damaging woolly bears.

Fearsome fact

Carpet beetles will also happily munch on seeds, nuts and pet food!

17

Skin-devouring mites

When you sink your head into your pillow every night, you might not be aware of all the activity inside it. Pillows, along with cushions and mattresses, can be home to thousands of tiny dust mites. Dust mites are short-legged relatives of spiders that feed on dead skin cells.

Skinny dust

Did you know that dead skin cells flake off from our bodies all the time? They are constantly replaced by new cells. The dead cells become part of household dust. The dust rains down all over our homes, but collects especially in pillows and mattresses. After all, we do spend one-third of our lives in bed!

Dust mites are so tiny they can blow into your house with dust.

Beast of the bed

Zooming in by at least 10x is the only way to see dust mites. They have eight legs, no eyes and long **chelicerae** (jaws) to chomp on cells. Dust mites like the warm, slightly moist environment in pillows and mattresses. In these conditions, dust mites breed fast. A female can lay up to 100 eggs during her 10-week lifespan.

A dust mite, artificially coloured green, feasts on skin cells.

This dust mite is **900 TIMES** its actual size

Other misbehaving mites

Several relatives of dust mites also live in or near homes, including flour mites, which live and feed in bags of flour. There are also straw itch mites, which can bite people handling straw or hay, leaving itchy red marks.

Fearsome fact

One-tenth of a typical pillow's weight is made up of dead dust mites and their droppings!

Paper-munching silverfish

Have the pages of some of your favourite books developed oddly shaped patches of paper, where the surface has been munched away? This is the work of the silverfish that live in dark, damp corners of many homes.

Glue for dinner!

Silverfish are flat, carrot-shaped insects without wings, around 1 cm (0.5 inches) long. They use their large antennae to find their way around in the dark and to smell food. They particularly enjoy eating wallpaper paste, and the glue that is used to hold books together, as well as paper and photos.

Know your foe
Silverfish move fast. If you turn a light on in a dark room where they are feeding, they will scuttle speedily into the shadows. They do this to stay out of sight of predators such as spiders and earwigs.

Silverfish are sleek and secretive insects.

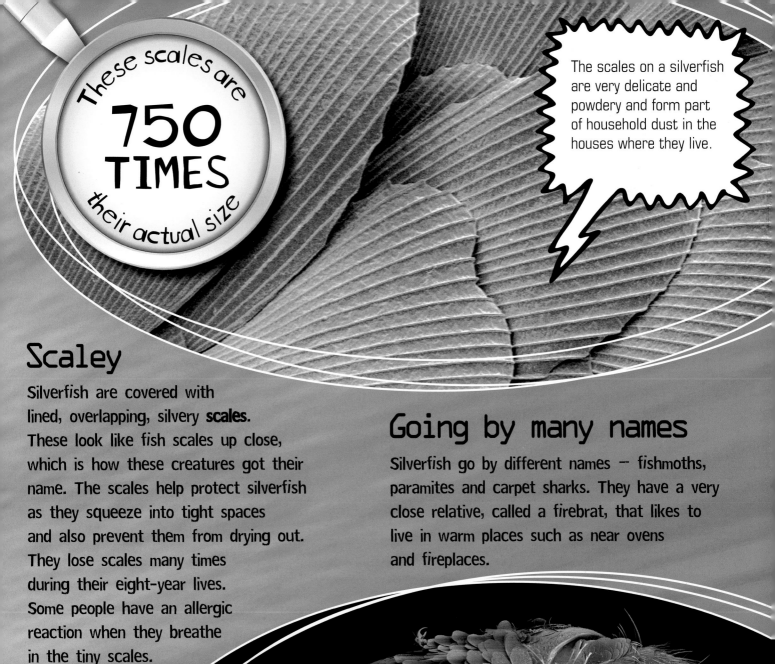

The scales on a silverfish are very delicate and powdery and form part of household dust in the houses where they live.

Scaley

Silverfish are covered with lined, overlapping, silvery **scales**. These look like fish scales up close, which is how these creatures got their name. The scales help protect silverfish as they squeeze into tight spaces and also prevent them from drying out. They lose scales many times during their eight-year lives. Some people have an allergic reaction when they breathe in the tiny scales.

Going by many names

Silverfish go by different names — fishmoths, paramites and carpet sharks. They have a very close relative, called a firebrat, that likes to live in warm places such as near ovens and fireplaces.

A silverfish, up close and personal!

Fearsome fact

A silverfish can survive a whole year without eating!

21

Nasty wasp nests

Wasp alert! Wasps live together in groups and build nests for their young. The trouble is that they often build nests in attics or other spaces in houses. A big nest can hold thousands and thousands of wasps, and they can sting people when they all leave the nest!

Paper houses

To make a nest, wasps scrape tiny bits of wood from trees, sheds and fence posts with their powerful **mandibles** (jaws). They chew this up and mix it with saliva to produce a paste. Then they use the paste to build the walls, ledges, tunnels and rooms of a nest.

Wasp warning

Bees sting only once but wasps can sting repeatedly. Wasp stings also give off a chemical that tells other wasps to attack, so don't swat a wasp near its nest or try to remove a wasp nest yourself. If you do, other wasps will join in the attack!

A wasp's nest has many little compartments where eggs can develop into adult wasps.

22

This wasp's mouth is **100 TIMES** its actual size

mandibles

This coloured SEM image shows a wasp's spongy tongue in red.

tongue

Wasp mouth at work

Zoom in on a wasp's mouth and you'll see something surprising! Wasps don't have a straw-shaped mouth like bees. Instead they have a short, bumpy tongue. They use this to lick up liquids like nectar and the juices of ripe fruit. Close up, you can also see the powerful mandibles that wasps use for grabbing, chopping and cutting things.

Fearsome fact

A wasp nest can contain 3000–5000 wasps and be as large as a beach ball!

Wiggly woodworms

Your home may be under attack! Are your chairs, tables or floors being eaten by woodworms? Look for tiny holes in wooden furniture or floorboards, and piles of wood dust next to them. These are the signs that woodworms are about.

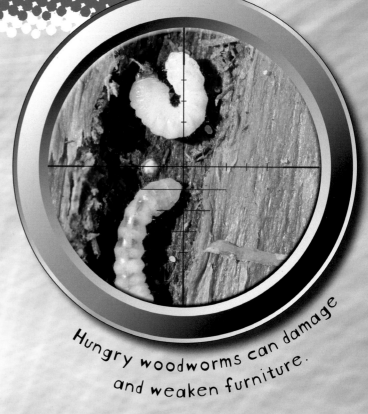

Hungry woodworms can damage and weaken furniture.

Adults that emerge from the wood are small, oval, brown beetles about 4–6 mm long.

Tunnelling terrors

Woodworms aren't worms at all. They are the larvae of the furniture beetle. Female furniture beetles lay their eggs in cracks in the wood. When long, wiggly larvae hatch out of the eggs, they start to eat their way down into the wood. They eat and eat until they are big enough to turn into adult beetles. Then they eat their way out of the wood. The adults fly off to lay more eggs, to produce more greedy woodworms!

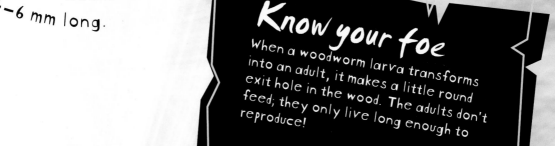

Know your foe
When a woodworm larva transforms into an adult, it makes a little round exit hole in the wood. The adults don't feed; they only live long enough to reproduce!

This woodworm larva is **120 TIMES** its actual size

A woodworm can live inside wood for up to four years.

mouth-parts

legs

Lousy larva

When you look at a woodworm up close, you can see it has three pairs of very small legs at the top of its body. It uses these to drag itself through its tunnels. It releases a special substance from its mouth-parts that helps to make wood soft and easier to eat.

Fearsome fact

Adult furniture beetles leave holes 2 mm across when they fly from wood. Longhornbeetle larvae leave holes five times wider!

25

Termite invaders

In some parts of the world, the most destructive pests are tiny and work in teams. Carpenter termites tunnel into the basements of homes to find wood to eat. If no one stops them, termites can demolish whole buildings!

Living together

Carpenter termites are insects that live in groups or **colonies**. There may be as many as 2 million termites in one colony! Most termites in a colony are workers. They build underground nests for the colony and search for wood to eat. They share the wood with the **queen**, who lays eggs in the nest, and other termites who look after the young and defend the colony from attackers.

A mud tube keeps termites moist and hidden from predators as they go in and out of a house.

Blind worker termites find food by following smell trails.

Wood shredders

Carpenter termites have white, soft bodies, and hard, jagged mandibles. They use these mandibles to saw off tiny pieces of wood the size of a grain of sand. When they chomp away the wood that supports a house, it can collapse!

Internal colony

Termites can only eat wood because of the even tinier animals that live in their stomachs. These digest the wood and release **nutrients** for the termites, in return for a safe place to live.

Timber! Termites can gradually destroy houses if they are not spotted soon enough.

Soldier termites have the biggest mandibles of all termites. They use these weapons to defend the colony.

Fearsome fact

Working together, a colony of termites can remove 400 g (13 ounces) of wood a day!

27

Glossary

allergic reaction when someone is badly affected by eating, touching or breathing in a substance, such as household dust or nuts

antennae pair of feelers on an insect's head that they use to feel and taste

asthma breathing difficulties resulting from an allergy

atom smallest unit of a chemical that can take part in a chemical reaction

bacteria simple, tiny living things that live in air, water, soil and within other living things

cell the smallest, most basic unit, from which all living things are made

chelicerae pointed mouth-parts of spiders and their relatives

colony group of animals that live together in the same place

digest break down food into small pieces that the body can absorb and use

fungus type of plant (such as mould) that usually grows on other plants or on rotting material

habitat area or environment where something (such as a plant or animal) lives

keratin type of tough protein that forms animal tissues such as skin, hair, nails and feathers

larva young that hatches from eggs of certain types of animals including insects, fish and frogs

lens curved piece of glass that bends light rays; used in microscopes and magnifying glasses

magnify make bigger; enlarge

mandible hard, cutting or crushing mouth-parts

micron unit of measurement equal to one-millionth of a metre; 50 microns is about half the width of a human hair

microscope device that produces enlarged images of objects that are normally too small to be seen

mould type of soft fungus that usually grows on damp surfaces

nectar sweet liquid made by plants to attract insects and other animals to spread their pollen

palp type of jointed soft mouth-part in animals (including insects and crabs)

paralyse make something unable to feel or move part or all of its body

pesticide chemical used to kill insects and other animals that are pests

pollen fine powder that forms in flowers and is carried to other flowers by insects

predator animal that hunts and eats other animals

prey animal that is hunted and eaten by other animals

proboscis tube-shaped mouth-part used for sucking up fluids such as nectar or blood

queen in insects such as ants, termites and bees, the queen is the largest individual in the group, which produces eggs

scales thin, overlapping plates covering the skin of many fish, reptiles and some insects

Find out more

Books

Do People Really Have Tiny Insects Living in Their Eyelashes?: And Other Questions about the Microscopic World (Is That a Fact?) by Melissa Stewart (Lerner, 2010)

Insect Investigators: Entomologists (Scientists at work) by Richard and Louise Spilsbury (Heinemann, 2008)

Micro-Organisms (Super Science) by Rob Colson (Franklin Watts, 2010)

Microscopic Scary Creatures by Ian Graham (Franklin Watts, 2009)

Spiders and Their Webs (Animal Homes) by L. Tagliaferro (Capstone, 2008)

Websites

Go to http://ag.arizona.edu/pubs/garden/mg/entomology/household.html to survey a wide range of household pests, divided up into the parts of the house they inhabit.

What do you know about spiders?
At http://www.earthlife.net/chelicerata/araneae.html you can fill in the gaps in your knowledge. Check out the different sections of the website, including Spiders and Man and A House Spider Safari, to learn the differences between the types of spiders you might find in your house.

Have you ever wondered about becoming an entomologist (someone who studies insects for a living)? If so, visit http://www.nhm.ac.uk/kids-only/ologist/entomologist/index.html for some ideas.

Discover some facts about cockroaches by visiting
http://www.nhm.ac.uk/kids-only/life/life-small/cockroaches/index.html

If you have enjoyed looking at close-ups in this book, you will probably enjoy the fantastic SEM images on display at
http://www5.pbrc.hawaii.edu/microangela/

Index

allergy, allergic reaction
   17, 19, 21
antenna 13, 20
asthma 9, 19
atom 7

bacteria 6, 7, 10
beetle   12, 16–17,
   24, 25

carpet beetle (woolly bear)
   16–17
cockroach 12–13
   furniture beetle 24, 25
   longhorn beetle 25
   museum beetle 16

cheese 8
chelicerae 19
cockroach 12–13

disease 12
dust mite 18–19

electron 7

flour mite 19
fly 10–11
   housefly 10–11

fungus 8–9
   mould 8–9
   mushroom 8, 9
   spore 9
   toadstool 8
furniture beetle 24, 25

habitat 6, 16
housefly 10–11

keratin 16

light microscope 7
longhorn beetle 25

mandible 22, 23, 27
microscope 6–7
   light microscope 7
   scanning electron
microscope (SEM) 7
mite 18–19
   dust mite 18–19
   flour mite 19
   straw itch mite 19
mould 8–9
   spore 9
mouth-parts
   chelicerae 19
   mandible 22, 23, 27
   proboscis 11
museum beetle 16
mushroom 8, 9

pesticide 17
pheromone 17
predator 14, 20, 26
proboscis 11

scanning electron
   microscope (SEM) 7
silverfish 20–21
skin cell 18–19
spider 14–15
spore 9
straw itch mite 19

termite 26–27
toadstool 8

wasp 22–23
woodworm 24–25
woolly bear (carpet beetle)
   16–17